DENIM JEANS

Wayne Jackman

Reading Consultant:
Diana Bentley
University of Reading

Commissioned photographs:
Chris Fairclough

Wayland

Our Clothes

Denim Jeans
Leather Shoes
Nylon Tracksuit
Plastic Raincoat
Woolly Hat

Editor: Janet De Saulles

First published in 1990 by
Wayland (Publishers) Ltd
61 Western Road, Hove
East Sussex, BN3 1JD, England

British Library Cataloguing in Publication Data
Jackman, Wayne
    Denim Jeans.
    1. Fabrics
    I. Title II. Fairclough, Chris III. Series
    677'.02864

    ISBN 1–85210–886–X

Phototypeset by Rachel Gibbs, Wayland
Printed and bound by Casterman S.A., Belgium

Contents

All the words that appear
in **bold** are explained in the
glossary on page 22.

Above *Pop stars such as Kylie Minogue often wear jeans.*

Opposite page *These children are wearing their favourite jeans.*

Have you got a pair of jeans?

All over the world there are thousands of people who have a pair of jeans. Millions of pairs are sold every year. All sorts of people wear them, kings, lorry drivers, pop stars and you.

Do you know how jeans are made? They are made from cotton. Cotton comes from plants and has been used to make clothes for more than 5,000 years! It is the most important clothing **fibre** in the world. The cotton which is used for denim jeans and jackets has been styled to make it strong and tough.

The cotton plant

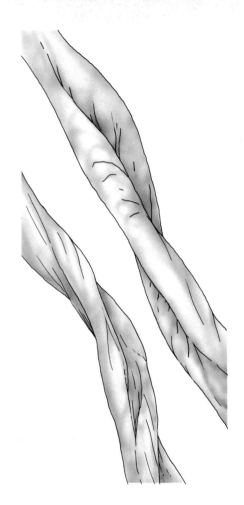

The cotton plant grows to about 170 cm. The best cotton is from the West Indies and is called Sea Island cotton. It is very fine and it has long fibres. Some types of cotton are not so good because they have short fibres.

Above *A close-up of some cotton fibres.*

Right *Jeans are fun to wear.*

Cotton is so useful for making clothes because it is very strong and hard-wearing. It can be washed often and at high temperatures without being harmed. It can soak up moisture such as sweat, and in summer it allows the heat from our bodies to pass through to the air, keeping us cool.

Above *Cotton clothes are comfortable to wear in hot places such as India.*

Growing the cotton

Below *The cotton plant in flower. When the flower dies the cotton fibres will grow.*

The small cotton plant **seedlings** must be looked after carefully so that weeds do not grow around them. Some farmers keep geese to eat the weeds. After about six months bright yellow or pink flowers bloom on the plants. These then turn into **husks** called **cotton bolls**. After another month the bolls split open to reveal the white cotton fibres. The cotton is then ready for picking.

In some countries cotton is picked by hand. This takes a long time. Picking by machine is much faster but a lot of extra waste such as leaves and dirt is also collected.

Above The picked cotton fibres will now be taken away and cleaned.

Left These cotton plants are ready to be picked.

Cleaning the cotton

The freshly picked cotton is cleaned in a **ginning machine**. This separates the cotton fibres from the seeds, husks and dirt. The cotton is then packed up and sent to a **cotton mill**.

Right Cotton fibres being tested for their strength. They must also be clean, and the right colour and length.

At the mill the cotton is once again cleaned and then it is **carded** and **combed**. This takes away the shortest fibres and sorts out the rest so that they all lie in the same direction. The fibres are then collected up into strands and stretched out. The strands are twisted, and finally spun together. The cotton ends up looking like very long, soft rope. This is called yarn.

Opposite page
Cotton can be dyed many colours.

Below *Denim being dyed indigo.*

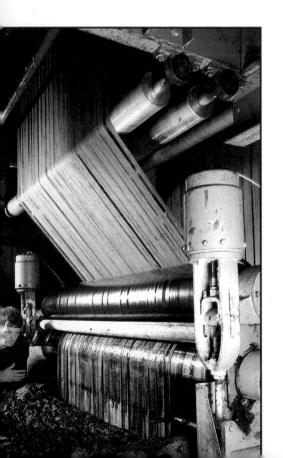

Dyeing the yarn

The white cotton yarn is then dyed a colour. To make the traditional blue of denim jeans a special dye called **indigo** is used. This comes from a plant which grows in India and which has been used as a dye for hundreds of years. Nowadays, the same colour can be made by using **chemicals**. The yarn is dyed as many as eight times. Indigo dye gradually washes out and our jeans fade. Has this ever happened to your jeans?

After being dyed, the yarn is **woven** into fabric on a loom. Dozens of different cotton fabrics can be woven – denim is only one of them!

The first pair of denim jeans

the cotton plant

A man called Levi Strauss invented jeans in the USA in the 1850s. He used a fabric named after Nimes, the town where the fabric was first made. This name gradually changed to denim.

picking

14

cleaning

Today our jeans still look like the earliest ones. The denim arrives at the factory and is carefully tested before being used. First of all the colour is checked. Then a small piece of denim is washed and rubbed many times to make sure that it will not shrink, wear out or rip.

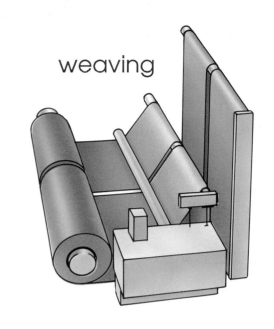

weaving

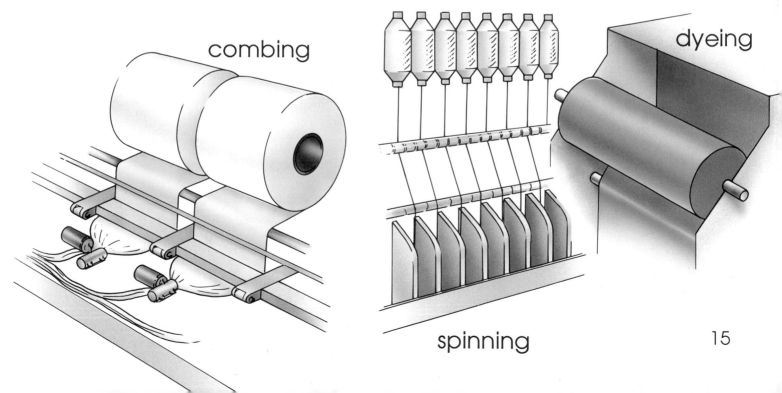

combing

spinning

dyeing

15

Cutting the denim

Once the denim has been carefully examined, it is cut into the many pieces needed to make the jeans. The people who do this are called cutters. The cutters use computers to help them make the different styles and sizes. It is important to waste as little denim as possible.

Above Patches on our jeans are both useful and fashionable.

Right These children are wearing jeans and jackets in many different sizes.

16

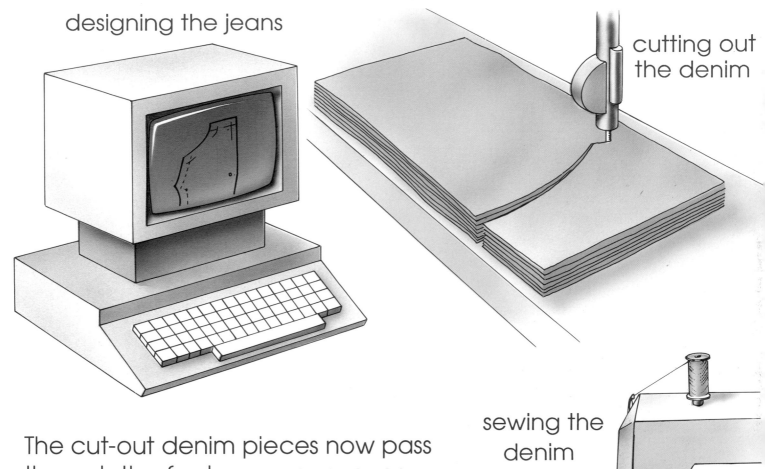

designing the jeans

cutting out the denim

sewing the denim

The cut-out denim pieces now pass through the factory on **conveyor belts**. The different sections are sewn together using fast sewing machines. One of the most difficult jobs is sewing the pockets.

17

Below *Because of their strength, jeans are good for working or playing.*

Jeans are made to be strong

Jeans are designed to be hard-wearing. Because of this, certain parts of the jeans need to be sewn together extra carefully. Have you ever noticed the small round metal pieces on the pocket corners of some jeans? These stop your pockets from tearing. The loops around the top of your jeans are sewn on with very close stitches. This stops them from breaking when a belt is put in and out of them.

Above Can you see the strong stitching on these belt-loops?

When each pair of jeans has been completely sewn together, one pair is taken out and is tested by washing and rubbing. When the inspector is satisfied, the rest of the jeans are sent to the shops. Your jeans should last for years – unless you grow out of them!

Above *This child is testing whether denim fades easily when it is washed.*

Look at your own jeans

Now have a look at your own pair of jeans. Can you find the places where they have been strengthened? If you have a pair of jeans which you do not wear anymore, ask an adult to help you cut out a small piece of the denim. Try soaking it in warm soapy water overnight. Has the colour faded at all?

Next time you are on a bus or in a queue, count the number of people wearing jeans. Denim jeans are probably the most widely worn type of clothing in the world!

Left *See how strong the pockets on your jeans are.*

Glossary

Carded   The short cotton fibres are taken out.

Chemicals   Substances used in chemistry. Bleach is a well-known chemical.

Combed   The long cotton fibres are straightened.

Conveyor belts   Long moving belts which carry things from one place to another.

Cotton bolls   These are the husks that the cotton flowers turn into.

Cotton mill   The factory where the cotton is cleaned, carded and combed.

Fibre   A little hair-like thread.

Ginning machine   A machine which traps the unwanted seeds and dirt.

Husks   The cotton flowers turn into husks after they have bloomed.

Indigo   A dye which has a purply-blue colour.

Seedlings   Baby plants.

Woven   When the cotton threads are passed in and out of each other to make material.

Books to read

Children's Clothes by Miriam Moss
   (Wayland, 1988)
How It's Made: Clothing and Footwear by
   Donald Clarke (Marshall Cavendish, 1978)
Levi Strauss Student Information Pack
Textiles by Stella Robinson (Wayland, 1983)

Index

Acknowledgements

The author and Publisher would like to thank the headteachers and staff of St Bernadette's School, Clapham Park, London, and of Middle Street School, Brighton, Sussex, for all their help in the production of this book.

They would also like to thank the following for allowing their photographs to be reproduced in this book: Duncan Raban 4; International Institute for Cotton 8, 9, 10; Smith and Nephew 11; Smith and Nephew and Paul Seheult 12; Zefa 9. The illustrations on pages 6, 14, 15 and 17 are by Janos Marffy.